Unit

Wonders of Nature

Mc
Graw
Hill
Education

Contents

Hap Hid the Ham

My dad had a hot ham.

Hap hid it.

Dad did not see it.
Dad had to sit.

4

Dad had a hot pan.
Dad had a tin can.

Hap hid the ham.
See it in my hat?

Hip Hop

Pam can see it.
It can hop.

Andrew Howe/Vetta/Getty Images, (inset) Tanya Constantine/Blend Images/Getty Images

It can sit.
It can see him.

It can see my mom.
It can hop a lot.

Can mom see it hop?
It can hop, hop, hop.

11

Hip hop!
It hid in a hat.

Ed and Ted Can Go On

Ed met Ted.
The men go on.

Ted can tap it.
Ed can tip a net.

Ed and Ted are hot.
Ed can sit and sip.

Ed can nap.
Ted can sit and sip.

Ted can tap it.
The men can go on.

Not a Pet!

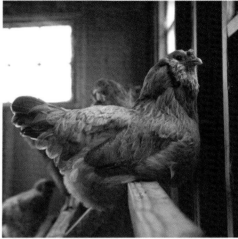

A hen can sit in it.
Not a pet!

J & C Sohns/
Picture Press/Getty Images

It can sit in a den.
Not a pet!

It can tap in a pen.
Not a pet!

It can sit in a pit.
Not a pet!

Ned Cat can nap.
You are my pet Ned!

Ron Ram

Can you see Ron Ram?
Ned can see Ron Ram.

Ned can go with Ron Ram.
He can sit on top.

Ron Ram can see a red fin.
Ned can dip a rod.

Ron Ram ran to it.
Can Ned pat it?

Ned and Ron Ram fed Ted.

Red and Ron

Red and Ron ran.
See Red with Ron.

sonyae/iStock/Getty Images

Ron fed a hen.
See a fat tan hen.

Ron fed a ram.
See a fit ram.

See a hot fat pig.
Ron had to fan it.

35

Ron had to rip it.
He fed Red.

Hap Hid the Ham WORD COUNT: 41

DECODABLE WORDS

Target Phonics Elements
Initial Consonant *h:* had, ham, Hap, hat, hid, hot

HIGH-FREQUENCY WORDS
my
Review: a, see, the, to

Hip Hop WORD COUNT: 43

DECODABLE WORDS

Target Phonics Elements
Initial Consonant *h:* hat, hid, him, hip, hop

HIGH-FREQUENCY WORDS
my
Review: a, see

Ed and Ted Can Go On WORD COUNT: 49

DECODABLE WORDS

Target Phonics Elements
Initial and Medial Vowel *e:* Ed, men, met, net, Ted

HIGH-FREQUENCY WORDS
are
Review: a, and, go

Not a Pet! WORD COUNT: 48

DECODABLE WORDS

Target Phonics Elements
Initial and Medial Vowel *e:* den, hen, pen, pet,

HIGH-FREQUENCY WORDS
are
Review: a, my, you

Ron Ram WORD COUNT: 50

DECODABLE WORDS

Target Phonics Elements
Initial Consonants *f* and *r:* fed, fin, ram, ran, red, rod, Ron

HIGH-FREQUENCY WORDS
he, with
Review: a, and, go, see, to, you

Red and Ron WORD COUNT: 46

DECODABLE WORDS

Target Phonics Elements
Initial Consonants *f* and *r:* fan, fat, fed, fit, ran, ram, Red, rip, Ron

HIGH-FREQUENCY WORDS
he, with
Review: a, and, see, to

37

HIGH-FREQUENCY WORDS TAUGHT TO DATE

Grade K

a
and
are
can
do
go
he
I
like
my
see
the
to
we
with
you

Initial and final consonant *m*; short *a*; initial *s*; initial and final consonant *p*; initial and final consonant *t*; initial and medial vowel *i*; initial and final consonant *n*; initial *c*; initial and medial vowel *o*; initial and final *d*; initial consonant *h*; initial and medial vowel *e*; initial consonants *f* and *r*